The 10 Principles

of

ENDLESS WEALTH

How to generate more money
than you can spend in a lifetime.

Copyright © 2000 2ndEmpireMedia llc.

All rights reserved.

No part of this work may be reproduced
in any form, or by any means, without
the permission of the publisher.
Exceptions are made for brief excerpts to
be used in published reviews.

Published by 2ndEmpireMedia.

**General Santos City
Philippines**

This publication is designed to provide accurate and authoritative information with regard to the subject matter covered. It is sold with the understanding that the publisher is not engaged in rendering legal, accounting, or other professional advice. If legal advice or other assistance is required, the services of a qualified professional person should be sought.

From a Declaration of Principles jointly adopted by a Committee of the American Bar Association and a Committee of Publishers and Associations.

This book is dedicated to those who believe there is more to life than they are currently living.

My hope is you will find inspiration as I have in the lessons contained in this book.

My mission in life is to pass the key that was handed to me when I needed it most on to others in the hope that they too, will be ready to receive it.

If you have faith as small as a mustard seed nothing will be impossible for you!

Matthew 17:20

All men and women are born, live, suffer and die; what distinguishes us one from another is our dreams, whether they be dreams about worldly or unworldly things, and what we do to make them come about... We do not choose to be born. We do not choose our parents. We do not choose our historical epoch, the country of our birth, or the immediate circumstances of our upbringing. We do not, most of us, choose to die; nor do we choose the time and conditions of our death. But within this realm of choicelessness, we do choose how we live".

-Joseph Epstein

Introduction
Beliefs
Learn From The Past
Seek Out Assets
Never Stop Learning
Reality –vs - Myth
Set Goals - Track Results
Invest For The Future
Live Below Your Means
Pick Your Seed
Dream, Plan & Do
Recap Of Principals

"A principle is the expression of perfection, and as imperfect beings like us cannot practice perfection, we devise every moment limits of its compromise in practice."

-Mohandas Gandhi

Introduction

There are millions of people who believe that they will never be able to achieve financial freedom let alone total independence and especially not right now in such seemingly poor economic times. And yet, there are many people that are doing just that as you read these words.

Right now, you can decide whether or not you will be among the people who get rich no matter what or if you will join the ranks of those who only wish that they could find a way but somehow never do.

The difference is subtle, yet powerful and it can be the difference between simply dreaming of more or actually getting what it is that you want. And that of course, would be to have more wealth and to live a rich and abundant lifestyle.

So, where do you find yourself?

Like most Americans I've spent my entire adult life chasing "*The almighty dollar*". It wasn't until I came to the realization that If I was ever going to make anything of myself I'd have to give up my old notions of what wealth was all about and start spending more time finding out just what the rich were doing that I wasn't. Once I started putting into action all that I had learned, my life began to rapidly change beyond my wildest dreams!

For over a decade now I've interviewed and studied some of the wealthiest as well as some of the most destitute society has to offer in order to extract the measurable differences in their opposing core principals.

In doing so I discovered many universal truths about wealth - how the rich acquire wealth and moreover how they keep it!

One thing became clear to me very early on. You must be willing to reconsider how you view yourself and your ability to make more money or to get rich. If you think that it will not happen for you, then guess what? That is exactly the result that you will get! You have to be able to change how you think and feel about yourself and your ability to get rich. This is critical

Remember that anyone can make themselves a success story. You do not have to be born into a certain class or be given an easy road to wealth. A quick look at the top 500 richest folks reveals very few wealthy people come by their money through inheritance. Most started out just like you and mastered the fundamentals you will learn in this book.

You will only get rich when you learn how to lay the correct foundation for growth and position yourself to attract the right opportunities into your life that will help you to achieve your financial goals. It's absolutely *that simple*

This book will provide you a framework to build your future on. The knowledge contained in this little book has aided in building MASSIVE FORTUNES so big that even the compounded interest handed down through multiple

generations would be hard to spend…
even over several lifetimes!

"As it is with the mastery of any skill however, the success is earned in the practice of the FUNDAMENTALS. I know you've heard it a thousand times before. But it's true - hard work pays off. If you want to be good, you have to practice, practice, practice. If you don't love something, then don't do it."

-Ray Bradbury

"A belief, however necessary it may be for the preservation of a species, has nothing to do with truth. The falseness of a judgment is not for us necessarily an objection to a judgment.

The question is to what extent it is life promoting, life-preserving, species preserving, perhaps even species cultivating. To recognize untruth as a condition of life--that certainly means resisting accustomed value feelings in a dangerous way; and a philosophy that risks this would by that token alone place itself beyond good and evil".

-Friedrich Nietzsche

Beliefs

You probably already know the old adage about having a wealth-oriented, positive mental attitude. And that is an absolute necessity. But it goes much deeper than that. In fact, you must dig right down to the very core of your entire belief system. Face it - everything you think you "know" has, in one way or another, been taught to you by someone else - parents, teachers, siblings, the media, associates, bosses. Rare is the individual whose beliefs are actually his own (which explains the rarity of truly wealthy people).

In essence, the person that you are is a person that has been created and molded by others - most of whom are probably not wealthy. These people may have had good intentions, and they probably even believe in what they taught you. But it's probably all wrong! This is the reason why 96% of all Americans retire without financial security and independence. It has nothing to do with money, and everything to do with knowledge, and the understanding of some basic truths.

Know this - money must not be your goal. It is only a tool, as will be explained at length in another chapter.

Right now, understand that your primary goal should be just this: to better yourself as a person, and to learn the basic truths.

Do this, and the money will come, not as a prize to be sought and coveted, but as an automatic by-product of the bettering of SELF. If you do nothing else, hammer this into your most basic and primitive beliefs!

Those who chase money for money's sake may, indeed, find it. But they won't be "wealthy". Wealth transcends mere money - it also includes good relationships with others, happiness, health and spiritual well-being. Being financially secure does not make you wealthy - it just makes you secure. Period.

Pick out any 100 Republicans at random and I'll bet at least 96 of them are Republicans because their Dads were Republicans. Pick out 100 Democrats at random - same odds. In short, you are not really you. You are a creation of others, molded in their image. So I ask you - if you are not the "you" that you are supposed to be, how can you expect to achieve the future that the real you wants and deserves? More to the point, if you share the belief structure of others who have not achieved wealth, how can you expect to fare any better?

Like a cake that is made up of certain ingredients, you are made up of your beliefs. They are your ingredients.

And if you have rotten ingredients, it will make a rotten cake. If the good folks who gave you your beliefs are not wealthy or happy, then it simply is not possible that the beliefs that they taught you will propel you into something better. Because if there is one truth, it is this: if you use the same recipe over and over, the results will be the same, over and over. The beliefs that kept them from wealth and happiness will also keep you from them, just the same.

Therefore, the importance of a proper belief structure is critical. I cannot and will not - tell you what you should believe, if I did you would simply be a product of my belief structure - you still will not have the confidence of knowing that your beliefs are yours and are founded by your own observations. But I will show you how to become the "you" that you should be, by showing you how to disassemble your old belief system and replace it with a better one, suited to you and your needs. This is a secret that, in one form or another, the wealthiest families such as the Rockefeller and Kennedy's teach their own children right from the cradle. And it is the first essential principal, so read on, learn and apply it, regardless of the cost to you.

To begin, grab paper and pencil (lots of paper) and begin writing down your basic beliefs. Jot down all those things upon which all your other beliefs are based upon. These might be your religious beliefs, your basic beliefs about money, family, friends and relationships, the opposite sex - any belief that is basic to survival as a human being. For example, you might write down that you are of the Christian faith, and you believe in the Christian God and in Jesus Christ. You might write that you believe "you can't fight City Hall (or the System)".

You may write that it takes money to make money, or that Republicans are this, or Democrats that. Be honest - if you believe it, write it.

Now, take one of those beliefs, and write it on a separate piece of paper. Jot down some reasons why you believe it. Who taught you this? What were the circumstances that led you to this belief? You may be surprised at the answers and discover something about yourself you never knew. It'll be a real eye opener. I promise.

Later when you get the opportunity, research the subject. Study it in books, or online. Delve into it. And as you study both the belief and contrary positions, try to pick out those things that actually make sense to you, and things that can be backed up with facts. Use such things to begin correctly structuring your beliefs.

If you have any belief in which you have even the slightest doubts, you absolutely must find some method of removing those doubts - or replacing the belief. Your beliefs are the very foundation of your existence. If they are weak, anything you build upon them will be in jeopardy. Your beliefs must be strong and unshakable, at least to you, even if they are laughable to others.

Never underestimate the power of belief - it is the basis of all miracles, religious or otherwise. The belief itself, and your complete faith in it is what gives you power to move mountains.

Now that I had a solid belief that was built upon my own research and understanding (yours may be different), I have since been able to believe in my God all the more, and I am all the more impressed with His work. And this solidity of belief (not necessarily the belief itself) has made me a better person.

As the parable goes, the house (life) you build can only be as solid as the ground (beliefs) you build it upon. And this is why it is so very important that your beliefs are yours, founded upon your own research. It is strongly recommended that, whenever you hit a "snag" in life, recognize that it is probably a case where your beliefs are in conflict with the reality. You then need to study those beliefs, and draw your own conclusions based on personal knowledge, not hearsay

Twice divorced and bankrupt Jim moved to Florida for six months, where he knew no one, and no one knew him. No one expected anything of him. He spent those six months discovering exactly who he was – studying his traits, his beliefs, and getting to know the person he was, as others see him.

He then determined what he would change, in order to become the person he wanted to be. Then he set about making these changes, simplified by the fact that no one there would expect him to be this or that. He cast out any belief that he could not verify with facts – at least to his own satisfaction. He built up new beliefs based on his studies. And when he left Florida, he was not the same man at all. Even his attitude and level of confidence had changed. A new love entered his life and his job prospects skyrocketed.

For the first time in his life, he was able to see exactly what he wanted from life. All confusion was gone, since he could now see things much more clearly. Where once he had been an agnostic, he now had a deep, abiding faith in a greater power. Where once he had been a bad tempered, angry soul, he was now a mellow, confident and smiling friend that people instinctively clung to. Where he had once been lost, he was now in charge of his own destiny. Jim admits it's amazing what clarity can do.

How can you tell if you need to reevaluate yourself?

If you are unhappy in your relationships, or they just are not working as they should, then a change is in order. If you are miserable in your job, and feel you could and should be doing something else, it is time to take a second look at your life.

If you get angry often, or find yourself less than tolerant with others, it is time to reevaluate yourself. If you cannot readily laugh and smile for no apparent reason, you should reconsider your beliefs. If you feel stressed much of the time, you may want to shrug off the old ways and climb into new ones. These are a few of the signs that tell you that there is conflict, and changes must be made.

Summary: If you are a product of your environment (as we all are at first), you must become a product of your own design. Otherwise, you will never be you. You will only be a compendium of others around you. And if you are not the "you" that you were meant to be, how can you expect to achieve happiness and wealth?

As children, we have no choice but to be molded by others. But once we become adults, we have a responsibility to ourselves to take charge of our own lives. If you do not make a conscious decision to redesign yourself and repair the damage, you will never succeed to the extent that you could have.

Reevaluate your beliefs, and make sure they belong to you, and that there is no doubt in your mind that you know the truth, at least to your complete satisfaction.

Nothing will do more to derail your attempts at success than to have your beliefs conflict with reality, or to have doubts in your own beliefs. If you cannot verify your beliefs to your complete satisfaction, cast them out and replace them with beliefs that you have proven to your own satisfaction.

Conflict has but one result - destruction. If your beliefs conflict with reality, you must change your beliefs.

By removing conflicts from your life, you will have an unobstructed road to travel. In short, if you question whether or not you are all that you can be, it is time to take a closer look as to why that is, and make the changes that need to be made. It won't happen by itself, and no one else can do it for you.

Decide about the person you want to be, then do whatever it takes to be that person.

Learn From The Past

We all know someone with an outdated haircut who listens to the "oldies" all the time. These people are clearly stuck in the past. In many more cases, however, there are individuals who, while they may not live in the past, they spend too much time reliving it, or dwelling on past events. Maybe you just can't get past that unfair boss who fired you two years ago. Or perhaps your life has been altered forever because you were rejected by a girl in the ninth grade. Or maybe you are still afraid of dogs because you had been bitten by one when you were four years old.

As mentioned in the last chapter, we are all affected to some extent by our past. Over this we have no control. But we do have control over how it affects us, and to what degree. The past cannot change. *But the past can change us.*

We have a choice as to what the past can do to - or for- our future. The past is the foundation upon which the future is built. So it is imperative that our past becomes concrete, rather than loose sand. But how can this be done, if the past cannot be changed? It is quite simple, really - it all revolves around how we perceive the past.

There is no past event that is single-sided. Each event has innumerable facets. Put ten people into a room and have them observe or participate in an event, then ask each one what they saw or felt. Every answer will be different - each of us will take something different away from an event.

Consider that modern history records Custer's last stand as *a massacre*, because Custer was white, and whites write the history books. But the Indians see it differently. Instead of a massacre, they see it as an act of self-defense against an invading force. To Americans, the people who brought down the World Trade Center were terrorists. To Osama bin Laden, they were heroic martyrs.

My point is this: while you cannot change the past, you can change how you perceive it, and therefore turn harmful events into positive acts that will strengthen your future. You can turn sand to concrete.

Take the child bitten by a dog. The child becomes an adult who is afraid of all dogs, simply because he never got around to viewing the event without bias and fear.

As a child, it is expected that a dog bite will instill instinctive fear of dogs. But as an adult, we need to reevaluate from a wiser perspective. We might then come to realize that only a very few dogs will bite, and most of those will bite only for what they perceive to be good reason.

We might discover that the dog had earlier been severely abused by a child, and now he views children as a real threat. When the child got too close, the dog may have felt he needed to defend himself (based on his own past events, and how he perceived them).

Realizing this, the fear of all dogs begins to subside, because we have reframed our experience with logic and a broader understanding. We now realize that a fear of dogs is irrational, and based solely on the single event that affected a child who was, at the time, not able to fully realize what was happening, or the events that led up to it.

If success is your goal, you must learn from the past, but not dwell on it. Each event should be a learning experience, and as adults it is our responsibility to insure that we learn as much as we can from each experience. If one man fails at something, he may feel hurt, embarrassed and demoralized, and quit.

Another man, failing at the same thing, might ask himself, "What can I learn from this"? Upon studying the failure, he discovers what went wrong, and tries again, which results in future success. And once again, how something is perceived has changed the ultimate outcome. The event was exactly the same. Only the result has changed because someone chose to dissect the event to discover the "why".

Case in point: Joe purchased a ski area. He lost a great deal of money and went bankrupt. He could have decided that he would never go into business again because he "obviously" did not have the sense for it.

Instead, Joe took the whole episode apart and studied it thoroughly to try and discover why he had failed. He realized that he had not been prepared for contingencies by having some extra capital available. Worse yet, he realized that he had purchased the ski area in April. It would be eight months before income would roll in. In the meantime, he still had to meet mortgage payments, property taxes etc. Joe determined that if he had simply waited until October to buy, he probably would have done well. Knowing this, Joe was better prepared to try again, and succeed.

What are some signs that you need to investigate past events - or even those in the present? Stress. Fear.

Failure. Giving up. Let's take a closer look at some of these "enemies" of success.

First, we need to decide if these "enemies" are truly enemies. We know that "giving up" is not conducive to success, and is an enemy - quitters never win. But what about stress, fear and failure?

Stress: Americans spend billions every year on medications to relieve stress. Experts tell us that stress is detrimental and can cause serious problems. So, it is an enemy, right? Wrong!

Contrary to belief, stress is a necessary survival tool designed to protect us from harm. Stress is to the human body as a smoke alarm is to a fire-prone building in the New York. It is a warning system. When a situation arises for which we are not adequately prepared for, stress results.

This stress is telling us that we need to be better prepared; that a learning experience is at hand, and we need to learn how to cope with it effectively. If we ignore this warning, stress becomes distress, and it is distress that causes us harm. Therefore, instead of trying to eliminate stress, we need to learn how to use stress to become better equipped to cope with situations, and in that way we eliminate the real enemy - distress.

Let's say Joe and Bill are both up for promotion at work. Joe has been learning and studying for the job, taking courses. He knows he is ready and capable of handling it. When he gets the promotion, there is no stress because there is no threat to his success – he knows the job.

Bill on the other hand has not studied, did not take the supervisor training classes in night school at the college, and is not prepared. He, too, gets the promotion, but is soon "lost" in the paperwork. His employees think he's a jerk. He starts fumbling, and the stress grows. He starts taking "three-martini" lunches, to quiet the stresses. His drinking and consistent bumbling on the job gets him fired, causing more stress.

All of this stress, which isn't being dealt with, becomes distress, and Bill finds himself in a downward spiral, out of control. If Bill had recognized the stress as a warning sign, he might have decided to buckle down and learn about the job. He might have taken those courses. This is what the stress was telling him to do. But he ignored it.

When stress appears, we have two choices:

- Ignore it, and head for the local tavern, letting the stress fester until it becomes distress, or

- Find out what is causing the stress, and then take whatever measures are necessary to remove the cause(s).

In most cases, stress can be removed either by getting more knowledge (education) which prepares you to cope with the situation, or by choosing an alternate direction.

It is not that difficult, really - if you are in a burning building and you run towards the flames, you will feel more heat (stress). So, turn and find another direction that reduces the heat. However, if you had been better prepared (by installing sprinklers, smoke alarms and fire extinguishers), you might not even have to face that situation in the first place.

When in a burning building, you can deal with it by either putting out the fire, or leaving the building - whichever one is most appropriate. It is the same with stressful situations.

In either case, you must learn to cope with stress by not ignoring it. Stress is trying to tell you something; that it's time to make a decision to learn, or leave. Wherever possible, learning is usually best, as it provides you with more tools from which to build success. But where learning is not enough, or cannot be done quickly enough, leave - change direction. THEN learn.

Failure: Success is created when we couple knowledge with effort.

The more knowledge and effort we put into something, the greater the chances are for success. That's simple enough. The trick, however, lies in gaining the knowledge in the first place. And we humans have a subversive knack for insisting on learning from our own experiences, rather than the experiences of those who have gone before. So experience is the precursor to knowledge.

So, how do we get experience? We get it from trying.

And when we try, we will either succeed or fail. In either case, we need to learn from the experience. If we succeed, find out why you succeeded, so the success can be replicated. And if you fail, find out why you failed, so you won't make the same mistake next time.

Each time we fail - and learn something from it - we get closer to success. Hence, failure is a valuable learning aid, and a good friend to those who seek success. I tolerate my failures because I know that in failing, I will learn how not to fail. Perhaps Thomas Edison said it best when he was asked about his great success in creating the electric light. He replied with the statement that he knew much more about failure than he knew about success. He stated that he had failed his way to success.

Fear: Nothing has done more to derail success than fear. Fear of failure, fear of success, fear of this or that. So fear is an enemy, right? Nope. You must know by now that things aren't always what they appear to be. We all have fears - the only difference between a successful person and one who fails lies in how each one copes with the fear.

Fear is a natural instinct for survival, and has the same basis as stress. It creates the "fight or flight" desire.

When in a state of fear, we choose to either fight, flee- or panic. The problem does not lie in feeling fear – it lies in choosing the wrong response.

Sometimes it is appropriate to flee; other times it is better to fight. But in no case is it appropriate to panic.

Panic is the only enemy here. "Panic" is to fear as "distress" is to stress - it is the result of not being able to cope with the situation, or to make the necessary choice.

Once again: Fear is good, panic is bad. Fear makes us act, or react. And success can only be ours through action. Panic is the certain fast-lane to failure. When faced with fear, determine the appropriate choice of action. If you decide to flee, that is fine, but you should then go forth to better arm yourself for the next time you face that fear. Then, when the next time comes, you are better equipped to fight and win.

Consider this as guerilla warfare. Fight when you can win, and flee when you can't. And if you flee, begin preparing to meet the enemy again, ready to fight and win. Learn what you need to learn, and do what you need to do in order to overcome that enemy the next time you meet, for it is certain that you will, indeed, face that fear once again. Otherwise you will spend your life in constant flight mode, never moving forward. A valuable lesson - in life, it is rare for anything to be as it appears.

Take pain, for example. Ask 100 people if pain is a good thing or a bad thing, most will state emphatically that it is a bad thing. But is it? Where would we be if we could not feel pain? "Extinct" would be an appropriate answer. If you cannot feel pain, you won't know there is a problem. Ignorance of the existence of a problem means you won't tend to it, or have a doctor check it out, resulting in something like bleeding to death, infection, disease.

The point is this: pain, like stress, is a warning, provided by nature and necessary for our survival. In my humble opinion, that makes pain a friend, not an enemy (albeit an uncomfortable, damnable friend to be sure).

Summary: Learn from the past, then put it behind you. The only things you should take from the past are positive memories and lessons learned. Everything else should stay where it is - in the past.

Let past and present experiences be reviewed and learned from, making you more capable of coping with fear, stress and failure. And start looking at fear, stress and failure as valued allies in your quest for success.

"The golden opportunity you are seeking is in yourself. It is not in your environment; it is not in luck or chance, or the help of others; it is in yourself alone."

-Orison Swett Marden

Seek Out Assets

The principal you are about to learn may well be the most important one of all. The concept is so simple and logical that most people overlook it. Don't make that mistake - if there is just one thing that is absolutely essential for sustained success, this is it!

It is important to realize one, simple fact – everything that exists is, to one degree or another, either an asset or a liability. Now it's true that many things have traits of both, such as a gun. On the one hand, if faced with threat of violence, a weapon in your possession would be an asset. But in the wrong hands (a mugger), it would be a liability.

Debts, while often called liabilities, can also be an asset. For example, you may owe on a mortgage (liability). But that debt proves to other creditors that you are creditworthy and responsible (asset), allowing you to obtain more credit when needed (big asset).

People are no different - each of us is both an asset and a liability to those around us. Some, such as Mother Theresa, are more of an asset than others (bin Laden comes to mind) who may be liabilities. But most of us are a rather ordinary mix of both.

The key to remember here is that the more of an asset you are, the greater your success will be. Conversely, the more of a liability you pose, the greater your chances of failing.

You may know that guy in town who is always grumpy, never has a decent word for anyone, keeps his yard looking like a junk yard and is generally an all-around pain in the butt. And you may notice he is a real nobody- a loser. No one would lift a finger for him in his time of need. No one wants to be around him. And no one will value him enough to give him a good stock tip.

How could he ever hope to get ahead when no one will even come near him?

On the other hand, we all know someone who is quick to help when needed, someone who is always pleasant and smiling. He/she just makes you feel good whenever they are around. You enjoy their company. And if this person is ever in trouble, everyone will be there to help.

Is it just a question of friendship? While that may be a part of it, it surely is not all of it. What is important is why and how such a person instills such good will in people.

First, however, we need to look at the benefits of being an asset.

Consider two used-car dealers, Bob and Carl.

Bob is a bit of a shyster, out for the quick sale. He uses pressure tactics. Once a sale is made, you never hear from him again, unless you make the mistake of going back someday. His cars are not properly maintained and always have problems, which he won't fix. Sure – Bob makes a lot of money at first. But sooner or later, folks catch on and go elsewhere, and Bob loses all he has worked for. Bob is more of a liability than an asset.

Carl, on the other hand is friendly and courteous. He talks about you and your family. He learns things about his customers, like birthdays and anniversaries. There is no pressure - he sincerely wants you to be happy with your choice. After the sale, Carl contacts you and asks how it's going, and lets you know that if you have problems, bring it in and he'll take care of you. You may get a card on your birthday or anniversary, letting you know that Carl really is interested in you, and cares.

After a while, all of those unhappy people who left Bob are buying their cars from Carl, and Carl's wealth grows. And Carl is not afraid to use some of that wealth to help others in need, either.

Something to ponder: What would happen if both Bob's house and Carl's house, which are side-by-side, burn to the ground. How many people do you suppose will rally around Bob and help him rebuild? How many around Carl?

Understand there is an important principle at work here: People like successful people (assets). They want to be around them, perhaps hoping it will "rub off". More importantly, people need successful people.

Successful people "protect" those around them, because they know it is those around them who have helped them to build wealth. By the same token, those around him understand that as long as they protect him, and keep him wealthy, he will be there to protect them from harm. On the other hand, most of us want nothing to do with people who pose a liability.

How much of an asset you are, and how many people you are an asset to, will determine the extent of your success. Bill Gates is tremendously successful because he is an asset to much of the world - it is through him that we all have computers that are relatively simple to use; computers that make our lives so much easier. Because Bill provides such a service, we keep throwing money at him

On the other hand, the local business owner at the computer store will only achieve a small portion of the success that Bill Gates enjoys. This is because his "asset allocation" is being limited to a local area.

Depending on the level of success you wish to achieve, understand that

1) You must be more of an asset than a liability,

2) You must be an asset to as many people as it takes to reach your desired level of success. If you want to beat Bill Gates, you will need to be an asset to the world. Otherwise, you may just want to be an asset to a few thousand people in your own community.

Summary: Be an asset to those around you - always. The greater the success you desire, the more of an asset you must be, to as many people as possible.

Remember - you enjoy your own assets. And so do other folks. If you are one of their assets, you fall under their protection, and they will cater to you and protect you, just as they would any of their other assets.

*"Education is not the filling of a pail,
but the lighting of a fire."*

-William Butler Yeats

Never Stop Learning

This principal has to do with education. But let's get something straight - education, in the sense of school and college is not education for purposes of achieving success. If this flies in the face of what you have been taught, that does not surprise me in the least. That is one of the reasons that 96% of all Americans never achieve wealth, even though 96% get a school education.

We are so engrossed in getting that formal education that we seldom get around to learning anything about money, wealth or happiness. It takes something more...

In addition to a formal education (formal education is more a memorization than a learning experience), each of us needs to do our own research and continue educating ourselves in those matters that concern us.

As I mentioned earlier, we must learn from failure, which means we must be willing to try a lot of new things. We must learn to investigate the relationship between cause and effect - if I do this, then that will happen. We need to be observant of everything around us, like a child exploring for the first time. We need to revive that feeling of awe and wonder when we encounter something new or different. But most of all,

We absolutely must attach emotions to these learning experiences.

The human mind is an amazing thing. But one thing is certain - we tend to remember things much easier and more clearly when it is associated with strong emotion. The emotion might be fear, sorrow, love, hate, awe – it doesn't matter, really, except that love and hate, being the strongest emotions, result in the things we seldom forget.

The important thing to remember is to get emotional when learning, even if that emotion is as simple as awe. Unfortunately, our society teaches us to keep our emotions in check. Perhaps this is one more reason why so many folks just never get to achieve wealth, they simply are not that emotionally invested in it.

Henry Ford quit school in the fourth grade. Abraham Lincoln never went to school at all. In fact, many of the more famous wealth builders and seekers of success throughout history never completed their formal schooling. But they did learn. They taught themselves those things they needed to know to complete their quest.

As Henry Ford once said, "I don't need to know anything except how to surround myself with people who know how to get the job done." He didn't need to know marketing - he hired marketers. He didn't need to know bookkeeping - he hired accountants.

I once heard about a man in Maine who has not had any schooling. He cannot read nor write. Yet he owns his own business, and has always been self-employed. So you see, there are different kinds of education. But the most important kind is that specific education you give to yourself by studying yourself, others, and the events around you. And like reading this book!

You will soon discover that your education is a progressive thing. You may determine, for instance, that you need to learn how to use a computer. As you do this, it just sort of leads into learning how to use a printer, scanner, CD burner... Eventually, it may lead you into creating a web page, then a website.

Then it's just a short hop into adding a shopping cart, downloadable info and creating electronic books for sale on the Internet. And the quest to create more books has you learning about new topics that you can write about. And the process, quite naturally, goes on and on.

If you keep yourself tuned into what you are learning and doing, and you have kept your imagination alive, you will forever be finding new opportunities for success.

Summary: Your real education begins after school, not in school. Never, ever stop learning. Learning is the substance that fuels growth, and growth is necessary for success.

"If money be not thy servant, it will be thy master. The covetous man cannot so properly be said to possess wealth, as that may be said to possess him".

-Francis Bacon

Reality –vs - Myth

What money is, and what it does, is probably not even closely related to what you think it is, or what you believe it does. I know that there are those among you who will say, "You're crazy!" Stick with me here.

Some people think money is nothing more than an evil necessity that was invented so we could buy all that great stuff we need and want. It is something you earn, then cash it in for all that neat stuff. A convenient form of barter. This is what we are taught, and this is what most people believe.

Some may go a bit further and say that, if you have any excess, you can invest it to make more wealth. Well, those people are a bit closer, but still off the mark. I'll explain in a moment. And here is another twist - a ton of money does not constitute wealth! Wealth is far more than piles of cash - it is an attitude, a state of mind and a way of life.

If you have ten million dollars, but you are unhappy, unfulfilled, bored, without spirit, without passion, without good friends, then you are not wealthy. You may be rich, but you lack true wealth. Wealth is a natural byproduct of the right lifestyle. If you live the right lifestyle, and have the right attitude and state of mind, money will come to you almost automatically.

Remember Carl, our friendly car salesman? His lifestyle, attitude and state of mind kept increasing the number of his customers, thereby increasing his wealth.

The money was nothing more than a byproduct of his chosen lifestyle. By being a great guy, people came to do business with him, and his wealth grew accordingly. We're getting close here, so pay attention. If you chase wealth, it will run from you, and evade you.

Wealth goes where it is deserved, not where it is wanted or needed. The other dealer, Bob, chased wealth, and ended up a loser. Carl, on the other hand, did not chase it - he simply let it come to him. The wealth chased him. Why?

Because any wealth that comes to you will be given to you by someone else. Someone who wants to do business with you. Before you can have wealth in your hand, someone else must place it there. It must come to you. And if you want people passing their cash into your account, you need to give them a good reason for doing so.

So now we are beginning to understand some pretty basic principles here, so let's take it one more step - what money does. Certainly, money buys a lot of things. But in and of itself, money has absolutely no value. The value is only perceived by those who have or want it.

Consider this: a man walks up to you and offers you a choice of either five million dollars or a Big Mac. Which one would you choose? Now let's say you are on a barren, desert island, starving, only inches from death. You find a bottle with a Genie in it, and he offers you a choice - five million dollars or a Big Mac. Now which one is worth more?

Perception and circumstances create value. And this brings us to the real power behind money: money is nothing more than a tool, like a hammer, a saw or a screwdriver. Ridiculous, you say? Ask yourself what you think a tool is, and what it does. Generally speaking, a tool is any object that is used primarily to construct something, or to change one thing into another.

Money builds empires. Everything we have that we pay money for is built with money. Money is a tool.

As such, a wealth seeker needs to realize that, like any other tool, it can only work for you if you keep it in your possession. If you trade your hammer in for a pizza, that hammer will now be working for someone else. And once you have eaten your pizza, you no longer have the pizza or the hammer. So, you need to hang onto as many tools as you can. Without tools, it is difficult, if not impossible, to build a future. OK, so we know money only has a perceived value, and it is an effective tool for building a better future.

The wealth seeker will realize that he can use that tool, and take advantage of the perceived value that others give it. He will invest that money, putting it to work earning more money. Businesses need that money, because its perceived value allows them to expand and profit. So, they borrow the money from investors (selling shares), and if all goes well, the investor receives a fair return on his investment. His tool is building a future. He leaves his profits in his investment portfolio, and now those funds are also making him money, and so on.

If you are beginning to get the complete picture, you will see that money must come to you because you live a lifestyle that attracts wealth (you are an asset). That wealth has a perceived value, and can be used as a tool to create more of the same (as long as you don't spend it - we'll get to that later, 'cuz we all have to eat). For now, try to remember *the guns and butter* theory.

Most people spend their extra money on "butter" items- things that make life a bit more fun. Luxury items. Then they grow old, and have nothing to show for it.

They can't even afford real butter on a Social Security check. But wealth seekers put their extra money into guns (investments). Once the wealth seeker has all the guns he needs, you had better believe he can get all the butter he wants, whenever he wants it!

Summary: Money is not wealth. Money is a tool. You can give it away to others, or you can put it to work building more wealth. Your choice. Choose well.

*"Before anything else, preparation is
the key to success".*

-Alexander Graham Bell

Set Goals - Track Results

It always amazes me that so many people are frustrated with being unable to get anywhere when they don't even know where they are now. I know that sounds absurd, but it's true. People want to get ahead, and reach certain goals. Yet they do not even know where they are starting from.

Every journey requires a starting point, a route, and a destination. If you have no idea where you are, how can you possibly plan a journey to a chosen destination? You wouldn't even know which direction to go in.

Therefore, before you start planning your journey to success, you need to know exactly where you stand right now. You need to take stock of your financial situation, your work, family, relationships - everything. You will need to know what your assets are, and what your liabilities are. And you need to be honest with yourself!

You need to know and evaluate every asset, because these will be your vehicle. You need to know your liabilities in order to plan your route in such a way that those liabilities do not become obstacles, or detours. Assets consist of more than just money, as you should know by now. Your friends and associates are assets.

Your family support is an asset. Your state of mind, even your friendly smile is an asset. Your skills, knowledge, training, hobbies - all of these are assets. And the same is true of liabilities - a bad temper is a liability, just like too much credit card debt is a liability.

To know where you stand, you will have to be painfully honest with yourself about such things. Evaluate them without bias. When you discover a weakness or liability, try to find ways to either overcome it, or turn it into an asset. How do you turn a liability into an asset?

Not long ago there was a real "geek" who dropped out of college. He looked, talked and acted like a geek. Who would have thought that he would turn his geekish nature into such a powerful presence that we know as Bill Gates, of Microsoft. He knew he was a geek. And he knew that he could use that to power his empire.

Everyone underestimated him, ignored him. This provided him with the powerful element of surprise, and he used that weapon with great precision. Before Steve Jobs of Apple - or anyone else - knew what was happening, it was too late.

If you cannot turn a liability into an asset, at least make sure it is under control. Do not allow anyone else the opportunity to use it as a weapon against you. As for your assets, while evaluating them, look for ways to make them stronger. And seek out ways to maximize them, and utilize their full potential. If you have trusted friends, call upon them to assist you. Seek their advice.

Let them try to punch holes in your plan - if they can, your enemies can, too. This shows you where your plan must be reinforced. Brainstorm with friends and family- even children. You will be surprised at the things a child's imagination can come up with. One man asked a classroom of first-graders what they would use strips of velcro for - he was fishing for ideas. One kid blurted out, "I'd glue 'em on my shoes because I can't tie my shoes yet." I think you can guess what the next hot product was in the stores.

Your computer is an asset, but are you using it to its full potential? Many of my businesses are web based. I consult with clients via email. I surf the web gathering up useful info on various topics that currently have my interest. It's like a library that's never closed.

Do you have a hobby that you are an expert on? People pay good money to learn from experts. Or maybe your hobby can produce income in some other way. If so, you can turn it into a part-time business that will put thousands of dollars in your pocket each year.

Summary: Spend some time finding out more about where you are. Make sure you know where all your money comes from, and where it goes. Know and evaluate all assets and liabilities, and maximize their potential. Once you know where you are, it becomes much easier to figure out how to get where you want to be.

"There's no reason people who work have to be resigned to situations and endure circumstances when we all possess the power to create better futures."

-John Renesch

Invest For The Future

You must realize that the road to financial security lies in investing for the future, and making your money grow. The difficult part for many lies in not having enough income to be able to invest. We will get to this later on, but for now let's take a closer look at why it is so essential, and exactly how it can create wealth. How much money is really needed, and where should you put it?

By now it is hoped that you truly understand and appreciate the "Guns & Butter" theory mentioned earlier. If you do, the rest will be made so much simpler. The basic premise is this: if you are willing to do for a little while what others are not willing to do, eventually you will be able to do all those things that the others can only dream about. In short, play now, pay dearly later, or pay a little now and play dearly later. Your choice. By going without some of those nice extras and putting that money to work, the day will come when you can have much nicer extras - all you want -

and not have to worry about paying for it later.

Understand this simple, yet ever-so-true principle: If you spend a dollar when you are 25 years old, you get one dollar in value (theoretically, anyway). A spent dollar is worth a dollar. But if you save and invest that dollar at 10% APR, when you retire that dollar will have grown to $48.

Putting this into perspective, a 25 year-old who spends $5000 that year on CD's, movies, pizza and other nonessential items has not spent $5000 - he has spent a whopping $240,000 worth of his future. If he spends $5000 per year for 4 1/2 years, he has blown over a million dollars out of his future. Ouch!

Try to imagine every dollar that you have spent since adulthood that didn't really need to be spent, but it was "fun at the time". Now just try to imagine all the millions you won't have because of those countless little flings. Chances are you no longer remember most of them, and no longer have anything to show for it all.

On the other hand, if that young man had invested those funds and waited until he was 39 to spend those dollars, two things would become apparent:

1) He will have a lot more money at his disposal.

2) Each dollar he spends will only cost his future $16 instead of $48. This is because it would only be growing for 28 years instead of 42 years.

By saving now and spending later, not only will you have much more, but that which you spend will provide greater value because it takes less from your future. At 10% per year, your money will double in seven years. At 15%, it will double in around 5 years. Hence, $10,000 invested at 15% at age 30 will grow to 1.28 million by age 65. As a seasoned real estate investor,

I have devised investment strategies that have been known to regularly yield from 100-600% per year, and in some cases, the yield is infinite because no cash is even invested, yet I get a good profit. Imagine getting a 600% yield on a $10,000 investment, even once! That would come to a whopping $60,000. And if you were to invest that $60,000 next year, again at 600%, your net worth would climb by $360,000. But what if you could profit $10,000 cash from a property in which you invested nothing? You would have an infinite yield.

Most of the techniques I have developed over my many years of investing do not require any cash or credit at all. I like that, because not only is the yield infinite, but it also leaves my working capital available for making even more profits on other investments. If you've never had access to large sums of money then numbers like these seem impossible. I assure you. They are the rule, not the exception.

A student of mine had made $16,000 cash in a single day, without investing a dime. He merely arranged to buy a property at one price, then resold it at the same time - all at the same closing. He needed no money, since his buyer was putting up the money.

He needed no credit because he was not going to hold this property. Really quite simple, and the recorded deeds, dated the same date for both the purchase and the sale make it easy to see how such huge yields can be made, even if you have no assets of your own.

Understand this one proven fact, however: nothing- not one thing - has made more millionaires out of ordinary people than real estate. Period!

In the face of this, you must realize the truth - if you do not go forth and create wealth for yourself, it isn't because you can't - it's because you won't! The individual who put this deal together and pocketed $16,000 was homeless and living in a beat-up van. He had no money, no job, no credit - *nothing*. Yet, he created wealth that day, from thin air.

So, if you still think you have an excuse for not building wealth or investing, I'd like to hear it.
There is nothing stopping you..... *except you*.

You should realize by now that a dollar saved today is more valuable than a dollar saved tomorrow (compounding interest that grows money). Conversely, a dollar spent today will cost you more than a dollar spent tomorrow.

But there is one more point here – a dollar spent at any time is worth less than a dollar saved at any time. So, if you like worth-less dollars, go ahead and spend 'em all, fast as you can. But if you are like me, you want to squeeze every bit of value out of a dollar that you possibly can. And that means saving and investing.

Later, I'll give you some pointers on how to find money to save and invest. For now, just understand that it is the only road to sustained wealth, and financial growth.

Summary: The surest road to growing wealth is through wise investing. And there are no excuses for not following that road.

"Why is there so much month left at the end of the money?"

-John Barrymore

Live Below Your Means

It seems that every father feels obligated to tell his children to "live within your means". Pretty good advice, on the surface. But there are two tiny little problems with that advice. If you live within your means, human nature being what it is, that's just like saying, *"Spend every dollar you make, and don't spend those you haven't made yet"*. And those are the problems. If you spend every buck, there's nothing left to invest. And if you don't spend money you haven't earned yet (use credit), you cannot maximize your earnings, and grow more wealth. Therefore, the way this advice should be worded is "live below your means, and if you use credit, use it wisely only for things that appreciate in value."

Money is not stagnant - it is always moving. Even when you put it in the bank, it moves as the bank invests it so they can pay you interest. Therefore, *if you aren't growing it, you're blowing it!*

Living below your means does not mean you must live in poverty. It simply means that you choose to not spend every dollar you make. It also means that you will use your intelligence, imagination and logic to find alternate ways of accomplishing things, at less cost.

Instead of spending $30 taking the family out to a movie with popcorn, spend $3 to rent a video and buy a box of microwave popcorn. You'll find the seating at home to be more comfortable, the movie entertaining, and the popcorn won't taste like buttered cardboard. You save money on the movies, money on gas, and you save time. Even once a month, this saves roughly $300 per year.

Living below your means (aka living wisely) means that instead of spending $7000 on a ski-mobile that you will use maybe four or five times each year, you would rent one for those times. You'll save thousands of dollars, and you won't need to house it, fix it, gas it up, pay for registration or pay the taxes on it.

There is time enough to own one after your future is secured and you need to find ways to get rid of some of your money. And even when you do buy one, you will have learned how to deduct it from your taxes (you'll learn stuff like this later). Sam Walton, who founded Wal-Mart and Sam's Club was noted for driving a '52 Chevy pickup truck. Rumor has it he could easily have afforded a few Rolls Royce autos, whereas he was the richest man in America.

When you see people driving a Mercedes and wearing a Rolex watch, you say, "Wow! He must have money." When I see someone driving a Mercedes and wearing a Rolex watch, I say, "Wow! He must have *had* money, but he has a lot less now."

Such things are status items, and status items are always prohibitively expensive, and are designed to separate a person from their wealth. I know a lot of people who want others to think they are rich (but they aren't - they are merely well off) who surround themselves with expensive status symbols. I also know some truly wealthy people, you would never know they are wealthy by looking at them. They drive a Chevy or a Ford, live in modest homes and dress casually.

Reason #1: By living modestly they save more money, which is then invested to make them even wealthier. They would rather have wealth than a Mercedes.

Consider: two people, each has $500,000. One buys a Mercedes for $60,000, the other buys a Ford Escort for $10,000. Each invests the balance of their money at 10%.

In ten years, the guy who bought the Escort will be $100,000 richer than the guy who bought the Mercedes. If the Mercedes guy also buys a $300,000 home, a Rolex watch and Italian shoes, while the Escort guy buys a $200,000 ranch, a Timex watch and gets his shoes at PayLess, the Escort guy will be more than two times wealthier than the Mercedes guy in ten years.

While the Mercedes guy is spending, the Escort guy is investing. You cannot earn wealth from money you spent!

Reason #2: When people see that you have money because you drive a

Mercedes or wear a Rolex, you become a target. Every sales person in the country will be approaching you and trying to sell you something. They can see that status is important to you, and if they have status items, they know you are an easy mark. Worse, unscrupulous people may file nuisance suits, just so you will settle, because it's cheaper to settle than to fight them.

Reason #3: The truly wealthy, if they are wise, have learned that the best things in life have little to do with money. In fact, money can actually get in the way of good friendships and community involvement. While people may respect your wealth, they may be a bit put off by it. They may assume that, being wealthy, you are also stand-offish when it comes to the "little people".

It's kind of like being the prettiest girl in school. You are so pretty that all the guys think they don't have a chance, so no one asks you out except for those dumb jocks who think they are God's gift to women.

Reason #4: When everyone knows you are wealthy, you can never be certain of a person's motives when they befriend you. Are they really a nice person, or are they just trying to get closer to your money? I know a man who had been quite successful, financially, and all of his romantic adventures went sour. It seems every girl he met was more interested in his bucks than in him.

Lonely and hurt, he decided to live and act like he was poor, but struggling to do better. Then when a gal showed interest, he knew it wasn't because of money. He married one of those gals, and as it turns out, despite having access to some pretty deep pockets, she still shops and bargain hunts as she always has.

Summary: The point, of course, is that your financial situation is best kept secret to some degree. Keep 'em guessing. By doing so, you become wealthier, and happier. Live below your means, but not to the point where you are giving up too much. Enjoy dessert, but remember that dessert doesn't have to be extravagant.

"For every man there comes that special moment when he is physically tapped on the shoulder and offered the chance to do a very special thing - unique to him and fitted to his talents.

What a tragedy if that moment finds him unprepared or unqualified for the work which would be his finest hour".

-Winston Churchill

Pick Your Seed

These next two are hardly "secrets". Everyone knows them. But what you may not know is that, taken alone, without the previous eight principals, they are nearly worthless. Having someone tell you these two secrets without telling you the other eight is like having someone tell you the punch line without first reciting the joke - you simply won't get it!

OK, so you've followed the first eight principals and you are ready to move on (of course, in real time the previous eight steps may take months to effect). You are now ready to find the method of getting from here to there. After all, you can't expect to sit in front of the tube watching CNN all day while the wealth just rolls in - this will happen later, when your money is doing all the work. But for now, the effort must be all yours.

Choosing a method may not be easy. You may need to find something that you feel comfortable with. Perhaps it will be something that relies on your specific skills or education. Then again, it may well be something that, for now, is totally unique to you.

I did not start out as a real estate investor. My education was in automotive design. My skills were as an artist and sculptor. Weird, huh? But after witnessing the sharp decline of the American auto industry from the inside, I realized that none of the above were capable of getting me where I wanted to go, in a reasonable period of time. Sure, engineering degrees can open doors to a great income, but a great income from working for a slowly dying corporation just wasn't good enough, and the stresses from all the competition and ladder climbing did not appeal to me. Nor did the backbiting, endless focus group thinking and hectic routines. I chose real estate partly because I understood it, and knew it was capable of creating huge wealth in a short time. I knew this because my parents worked for investors. I knew, too, that real estate was the one career that did not require a costly education, and anyone could do it, as long as they were willing to learn the basic ins and outs. And I also knew that you don't need money or credit to get started. Since I had neither, at first, I was certainly well qualified!

You may want to consider real estate, yourself, for some of those same reasons. Or, you may decide to choose consulting in your area of expertise, or writing books, or marketing products. You may simply decide to turn a hobby into a moneymaking business. Frankly, there are almost as many methods as there are people.

So how do you discover your method? If you have followed the previous eight steps, you should already have a fair idea of some possibilities. In the section about discovering and evaluating your assets, you may have found an opportunity that you hadn't thought of before. Keeping an open mind, letting your imagination run free and learning new things are the keys to uncovering your method.

Which method you choose may be determined by your needs and goals. For example, if your goal is to get there fast and solid, you might choose to learn how to invest in real estate. You certainly would not choose a method that only increases your net worth by 10% a year. If your goal is to have your name become a household word, you may choose something that has potential to be high profile, like authoring a best seller.

Only you can choose your goals, and determine which method is best suited for achieving those goals, based on the assets you have available to you or the assets you can get your hands on, such as books that will teach you what you need to know.

If you do not have a college education, you would probably not consider choosing a method that relies heavily on a diploma. If you do not like crowds, you would avoid methods that place you into crowded situations. If you love the limelight, you may consider a method that puts you up on stage, and takes advantage of your winning smile. In all truth, the method does not matter much, except that it fills your needs and you can learn to enjoy it, and it suits you.

If you find yourself having difficulty choosing a suitable method, try making a list of all your assets, skills, training, special knowledge, likes and dislikes.

Then ask friends and relatives what they think would fit nicely, based on that list. This is pretty much what those aptitude tests do - they find out what you like, and what your strengths are, then determine what careers might be best suited for you.

Brainstorm with people you know and respect. Make a game of it, so your friends can do the same. Maybe some of them will profit, as well. The more people in your circle who profit and succeed, the more your own wealth will grow. After all, how are you ever going to attract any money away from people who don't have any?

Help others to prosper, and you become valuable to them, to the point that they will try to help you prosper. In this way, both of you enjoy greater wealth. If you can't make any money from the poor, then you should work to help them prosper. And now that they have money, you can bring more of it home yourself.

It's like planting corn - if you plant a single kernel, it will grow and produce about 1000 kernels. You eat 900 of those kernels, and plant the remaining 100, which in turn will produce 100,000 kernels. And so it goes. Before long you are producing so much corn that you are selling all the excess, turning it into more money, which can then purchase more seed for other crops. You grow and prosper. And there is enough food for everyone.

Summary: Choose a method to take you where you want to go. And assist others in getting there, too, so more wealth is made available to you, and you gain the "protection" of others who value your contributions to their own futures.

Every choice moves us closer to or farther away from something.

Where are your choices taking your life? What do your behaviors demonstrate that you are saying yes or no to in life?

-<u>Eric Allenbaugh</u>

"Do not depend on the hope of results. You may have to face the fact that your work will be apparently worthless and even achieve no result at all, if not perhaps results opposite to what you expect. As you get used to this idea, you start more and more to concentrate not on the results, but on the value, the rightness, the truth of the work itself. You gradually struggle less and less for an idea and more and more for specific people. In the end, it is the reality of personal relationship that saves everything."

-Thomas Merton

Dream, Plan & Do

Like the previous advice, this one is well-known, but seldom followed. Simply put, you must first dream it, then plan it, then do it. It is virtually impossible to succeed any other way.

You cannot expect to put a plan into action if there is no plan. And if you act without a plan, it is doomed from the start. Furthermore, you cannot devise a solid plan if you have not already dreamed an idea upon which a plan is put together.

Unfortunately, our society quashes dreamers. They laugh at them, and belittle their dreams. So most people have given up dreaming. What a shame. Since a dream is the first step toward accomplishing anything, forget about those other people and go ahead and dream. Dream big! Really big! Bigger than you honestly ever expect to achieve. Why? Simple mathematics and trajectory (physics), following the laws of nature.

Have you ever shot an arrow, or fired a gun? Whenever you aim at a target, you must aim high, to allow for trajectory - the natural drop that occurs because of gravitational force. And even in life, while seeking wealth and aiming for a goal, there are forces at work that will create a trajectory. There will be obstacles. There will be detours as the unexpected pops up. So, if you want to get to the top of the mountain, you must aim for the moon. Aim high when you dream and plan, or I guarantee you will fall short, and be disappointed.

I can't give you any directions on dreaming (everyone has different goals), but I can tell you this: it is only the first phase. There must come a time when you stop dreaming long enough to put together a plan, then work that plan. Don't dream your life away - You must act on those dreams.

As far as planning is concerned, however, I have a very definite advice for you. Hold tight, as this will fly in the face of conventional thought, but after you read it, and really think about it, you will probably come to the sudden realization that it is the only way that can work. No wonder all those other plans aren't getting you anywhere!

Two words: PLAN BACKWARDS. Pretty dumb, eh? But think about the situation for a moment. You are here. You want to be there. You need to plan a route, an itinerary of sorts.

Conventional wisdom dictates that you put one foot in front of the other until you get there. Sounds logical enough - if you're going on vacation or something. But life's goals are different - everyone has different goals. You simply cannot say, "OK, I'll do this today, and that tomorrow, and eventually I will get to that goal." Why not? Because life does not follow a mathematical plan. It is not a smooth function. There are obstacles, detours, enemies, and a bunch more Indians than Custer had ever imagined. THAT is life. Deal with it!

Your first step is not to plan what to do today. Your first step is to determine exactly where you want to be, and when. This is because, if you want to go to L.A. for a certain ball game, it just isn't good enough to simply reach L.A. You must reach it on time. The purpose of the journey is crucial. So, let's say you want to have a net worth of "X" dollars in ten years. Be specific.

The average person would then go about making a plan, starting with what he will do today to get started. That's completely wrong! Since he has no way of knowing if that first step is sufficient for having "X" in ten years, he is just guessing and hoping. As a serious wealth builder, you would do it backwards. Your plan would go something like this (simplified, for purposes of the example): In 10 years I'll have $X in net worth.

Assuming I can make my wealth grow at a rate of 25% per year (bear with me a moment), this means I will need to reach 4/5 of $X in 9 years, which we will call $Y. And in order to have $Y in 9 years, I will need to have accumulated 4/5 of $Y in 8 years, which equals $Z. You would keep following it backward until you get to the here and now - what would you need right now, so at 25% per year it would grow to $X in 10 years. THAT my friend, is your first step.

Now you're saying, "Hey, where the heck would I come up with a lot of money today, and how could I earn 25% a year?" The answer is: Real estate - 97% of all millionaires made their fortunes in real estate. Allow me to blow your mind.... Let's say that, by one of any number of ways you can get your hands on $3000 or so (This is a worst case scenario. I've done hundreds of deals for just a simple $1 bill by adding an intangible value or trade for something else as well!)

You could option a $150,000 property and easily make 10% profit, or $15,000. After taxes, maybe you would net only $10,000 or so. And let's say you only do this once this just once a year. You now have $10,000 plus your original $3000 investment back - $13,000. That's more than a 400% return (not just that measly 25%)! Therefore, you could easily reach your goal when your yield is so high. That is the power of knowledge in real estate, which is why I chose it for my primary career.

So, if you know exactly where you want to be, and plan backwards, you will know exactly what you must do - and what you must have - at each step of the way. This is how wealth works, and since it is wealth you are after, get used to planning things backward. In more real terms, let's say your goal is to be a successful veterinarian in "X" years. You would have to work backwards to determine at exactly what point you must graduate from college, then backwards to see how many credits you must earn each year to accomplish that (assuming night school, at your convenience). If you were to plan forward, and simply guess what you must accomplish by any certain point, you would most assuredly miss the mark, and it might take many more years to be that veterinarian.

Plan Backwards. It's the only way that works. Once your plan tells you what you must accomplish in one year, You need to break that year into quarters, then break the first quarter into weeks, and the first week into days, so you know exactly what you must do today. And as each new week approaches, you must also break that down into days. When planning, don't forget common sense.

Think of your goal as an elephant, and your plan is to eat that elephant. You can't just pull up a chair, grab the A-1 and start eating that mammoth - you just can't do it! It's too big! Instead, you would 1) take said elephant to local butcher guy, 2) after his shock and laughter subside, have local butcher guy cut your elephant up into steaks, chops & burger, 3) put it in your freezer (if you don't have one, getting one would be step 2), and 4), eat a burger or chop or steak every day, until you have eaten that elephant.

If you need to eat the elephant by a certain date, determine how much pachyderm you gotta stuff down your throat each day by planning backwards. Then pass the A-1! (Detours happen. Include contingencies in your plan, such as a BBQ for all your friends). If you think you will need to have fish or chicken once a week, for variety, then make sure you calculate those lost days into your plan, and eat more beef on those days you eat "on task". Now that you have a plan, you must work the plan; put it into motion. This is where you will need some logic and common sense, as well as drive, determination, ambition, persistence.

Keep a daily calendar, or journal. Have it in writing as to exactly what you must accomplish each day, and try not to go to bed at night without having done it. Don't worry if you fall a bit behind, so long as you catch it up in the next day or so. If these "behind" things grow too much, like credit bills, they will get out of hand and you won't be able to catch up. Then you can kiss your goal bye-bye, or at the very least you will have to reschedule it. So plan wisely, and break things up into bite-sized pieces. Do not try to take on too much at once.

Each night before bed, I write down the things I must do tomorrow. In the morning, before even getting dressed, I read that to-do list again. Now for some grand advice - tackle the hardest, dirtiest, ugliest tasks first. You are fresher in the morning – not all worn out from a day's work. Better yet, by getting those nasty ones out of the way early, it is much easier to look forward to the rest of the day. The rest of the day will be a piece of cake, and you can end the day on a good note, which helps keep you in the state of mind that really is crucial for building wealth. And don't think you have to do it all by yourself. Don't be afraid to enlist some help when needed. It is better to give up some cash than to fall behind schedule. I have come to the realization that money is a replaceable resource - time is not!

Once you lose a minute, it's gone forever, and cannot be replaced. If given a choice between losing time or losing money, I will always opt for losing the money. Because if I have time, I can make more money. But having money cannot buy me more time. I do not allow myself to retire at night until I have, at the very least, made some progress toward my goals. And my goals are always in a state of flux - liquid- ready to be changed at a moment's notice. I do this because things change, and I change. I may set a goal for ten years in the future, and in three years I may discover something that "out dates" my previous goal.

Summary: Plan your work; work your plan. Plan in reverse to insure success rather than wide shotgun blast forward movements. And remain flexible, because life is not stagnant.

Recap Of Principals

#1: If you are a product of your environment (as we all are at first), you must become a product of your own design. Otherwise, you will never be you. You will only be a compendium of others around you. And if you are not the "you" that you were meant to be, how can you expect to achieve happiness and wealth? As children, we have no choice but to be molded by others. But once we become adults, we have a responsibility to ourselves to take charge of our own lives and pursue our own reality.

If you do not make a conscious decision to redesign yourself and repair the damage, you will never succeed to the extent that you could have. Reevaluate your beliefs, and make sure they belong to you, and that there is no doubt in your mind that you know the truth, at least to your complete satisfaction. Nothing will do more to derail your attempts at success than to have your beliefs conflict with reality, or to have doubts in your own beliefs. If you cannot verify your beliefs to your complete satisfaction, cast them out and replace them with beliefs that you have proven to your own satisfaction.

Conflict generates one result - destruction. If your beliefs conflict with reality, you must change your beliefs. By removing conflicts from your life, you will have a clear road to travel. In short, if you question whether or not you are all that you can be, it is time to take a closer look as to why that is, and make the changes that need to be made. It won't happen by itself, and no one else can do it for you. Decide the person you want to be, then do whatever it takes to be that person.

#2: Learn from the past, then put it behind you. The only things you should take from the past are good memories and lessons learned. Everything else should stay where it is - in the past. Let past and present experiences be reviewed and learned from, making you more capable of coping with fear, stress and failure. And start looking at fear, stress and failure as valuable allies in your quest for success.

#3: Be an asset to those around you - always. The greater the success you desire, the more of an asset you must be, to as many people as possible. Remember - you enjoy your own assets. And so do other folks. If you are one of their assets, you fall under their protection, and they will cater to you, just as they would any of their other assets.

#4: Your real education begins after school, not in school. Never, ever stop learning. Learning is the substance that fuels growth, and growth is necessary for

#5: Money is not wealth. Money is a tool. You can give it away to others, or you can put it to work building more wealth. Your choice. Choose well.

#6: Spend some time finding out more about where you are. Make sure you know where all your money comes from, and where it goes. Know and evaluate all assets and liabilities, and maximize their potential. Once you know where you are, it becomes much easier to figure out how to get where you want to be.

#7: The surest road to growing wealth is through wise investing. And there are no excuses for not following that road. Think about it - when you want to get somewhere fast do you take back roads or highways? If you get lost along the way there are plenty of people who have gone before you. Ask for directions!

#8: Your financial situation is best kept secret to some degree. Keep 'em guessing. By doing so, you become wealthier, and happier. Live below your means, but not to the point where you are giving up too much. Enjoy dessert, but remember that dessert doesn't have to be extravagant.

#9: Choose a method to take you where you are going. And assist others in getting there, too, so more wealth is made available to you, and you gain the "protection" of others who value your contributions to their own futures.

#10: Action generates results. Plan the work; work the plan. Plan in reverse to insure success rather than willy-nilly forward movement. And remain flexible, because life is not stagnant.

Lastly, it's my hope you forge for yourself the life you dream of. Don't wait for it to come to you. Go get it!

"A lobster, when left high and dry among the rock, does not have the sense enough to work his way back to the sea, but waits for the sea to come to him. If it does not come, he remains where he is and dies, although the slightest effort would enable him to reach the waves, which are perhaps within a yard of him.

The world is full of human lobsters; people stranded on the rocks of indecision and procrastination, who, instead of putting forth their own energies, are waiting for some grand billow of good fortune to set them afloat".

-Orison Swett Marden

About the Author:

Dan Howe is the author of the wildly successful POWER PROFITS!™ series as well as several other works ranging from real estate and investing to advanced marketing and life strategy coaching for the financially challenged entrepreneur. He is a nationally recognized speaker and frequently appears on financial radio and television programs throughout the USA and Canada.

Dan practices what he preaches. He is is the founder of eight companies, all started with no money up front and each boasting amazing growth and sustainability. He currently lives in the Philippines and travels around the world to spread his message.

To book Dan as a featured speaker at your next business conference contact us at

Whamtrade@rocketmail.com for details and scheduling. Or visit us at

2ndEmpireMedia.com

www.ingramcontent.com/pod-product-compliance
Lightning Source LLC
Chambersburg PA
CBHW051727170526
45167CB00002B/837